LifeKeys

DISCOVERY WORKBOOK

DISCOVERING...
WHO YOU ARE • WHY YOU'RE HERE • WHAT YOU DO BEST

JANE A.G. KISE
DAVID STARK
SANDRA KREBS HIRSH

BETHANY HOUSE PUBLISHERS
MINNEAPOLIS, MINNESOTA 55438

Introduction

LIFEKEY 1

God has an important part for you—yes, YOU—to play!

The book *LifeKeys* grew out of our efforts to help members of our church find meaning and purpose through discovering and affirming

- **What they do best** (life gifts and spiritual gifts)
- **The places or atmospheres that give them the most energy** (personality type and values)
- **The purposes God placed in their hearts** (passions).

These truths about *who you are, why you're here,* and *what you do best* can help you find personal pathways to fulfilling work, activities, and opportunities for service.

This *LifeKeys Discovery Workbook* offers you a personal, concise way to capture your LifeKeys. We encourage you to use this in conjunction with the full *LifeKeys* book and suggest you date this booklet and place it where you can refer to it often to renew your commitment to live the life for which God designed you. For we believe

- **Each human being is created in the image of God** (Genesis 1:26-27). We hope that through the *LifeKeys* process, you will come to appreciate the significance of the fact that somewhere inside you is *the image of God,* particularly if you view yourself or your gifts and talents as insignificant.

- **You were created with a unique, specially chosen blend of gifts** (Psalm 139:13-16). God gave you everything you need—the truly right gifts chosen just for you. If you struggle to understand how those gifts mesh or how they might be used, we hope that through the *LifeKeys* process, you might discover the purposes or settings that will clarify the merit of your gifts.

- **God has in mind specific good works for you to accomplish** (Ephesians 2:10). If you have yet to be a part of the ventures God has in mind for you, a rich experience awaits you. However, you need to discover that niche—the niche that God promises us is there.

Join us in the process of *LifeKeys* and allow yourself to uncover your gifts, personality, values, and passions—the person that God meant you to be. Place before yourself the wonderful truth that somewhere deep inside of you is a person designed by God. You can find no path more fulfilling than the one that uses your unique gifts as God intended.

LifeKey 2

Doing what comes naturally is part of God's plan.

Proverbs 22:6 tells us: *"Train up [children] in the way [they] should go [and in keeping with their individual gift or bent], and when [they are] old [they] will not depart from it"* (Amplified Bible).

Each one of us has a right way to go—a natural bent. This way is different for everyone. While many of us are in careers or situations that utilize our life gifts well, some of us—either because of uninformed choices, expediency, or the wishes of others—are in positions that are a poor fit.

Let's take a fresh look at the things you do that energize you, where your interests lie—your natural bent. For more than seventy years many people have found answers through theories of career choices, particularly those of John Holland. His theory postulates that the world of work can be broken into six areas of preference—that is, six areas in which people tend to cluster as they look for fulfillment by using their life gifts. Holland labeled these areas Realistic [R], Investigative [I], Artistic [A], Social [S], Enterprising [E], and Conventional [C]. People who have similar interests or life gifts tend to enjoy similar work environments *and* want to work in places where they can follow their natural bent.

Holland pictured the relationships among these areas by diagramming them as a hexagon. Typically, people are a blend of two and often three of the six areas, adding richness to the workplace. Often these two or three areas are next to each other on the hexa-

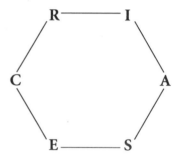

gon, although it is just as normal for people to have interest patterns that are exactly opposite each other on the hexagon. Take some time to explore the descriptions of each area to see which sound like you. These are the "home fields" where you can begin the process of identifying your life gifts. Not everyone has all of the life gifts listed under each area. In addition, someone can have life gifts in areas other than his or her home field. Your interest theme, though, is a great place to start the search for your natural bent.

Beginning with the pages for the areas you identify as your natural bent, answer the questions for those gifts you believe to be your life gifts. Then continue through the interest areas in their order of priority to you.

The Realistic Type

General Description:

- **Outdoors-oriented—dislike being desk-bound**
- **Mechanical—enjoy making, fixing, and working with things and machinery**
- **Physically coordinated—may be athletic or possess motor skills**
- **Hands-on—take a concrete approach to solving problems**

In their spare time, Realistic types like to enjoy the out-of-doors, even if they spend that time attending to home maintenance tasks. Many own recreational vehicles, sporting goods, and whatever tools they might need to get the job done.

With these characteristics, many Realistic types volunteer for maintenance projects, outdoor activities, providing transportation, building, or other tangible projects.

REALISTIC LIFE GIFTS

Life Gifts	When have I used this? Or have I dreamed about using this?	How enjoyable were these experiences (1=terrible, 10=great)	How easy or difficult is it for me to use?	Could this be a life gift?
Mechanical aptitude—able to understand and apply the principles of mechanics/physics				
Operating heavy equipment, driving, piloting—construction equipment as well as transportation vehicles				
Manual dexterity—skill and ease at using one's hands or fine tools				
Building mechanical/ structural devices—able to design and/or assemble materials as well as execute repairs				
Physical coordination—using multiple muscle movements to a single end, such as needed in athletics, skilled trades, etc.				
Organizing supplies or implements—able to identify methods that lead to ease of retrieval and maintenance				
Taking physical risks—attracted to activities or occupations with elements of physical danger				
Emotional stability, reliability—able to react impersonally to situations and thereby stay on course				

The Investigative Type

General Description:

- **Curious—tend to be observers, critics of their surroundings who try to understand "why?"**
- **Rational—apply scientific, strategic perspectives**
- **Intellectual—enjoy solving problems through an analytical, scholarly approach**
- **Introspective—would rather create, working alone on abstract ideas, than implement solutions**

Investigative types typically choose hobbies that involve complex activities such as skiing, mountain climbing, spelunking, or sailing, where technology and skill play major roles. If they own a computer, they know how it works and how to optimize its performance. For Investigative types, work and play are often one and the same.

With these characteristics, Investigative types might volunteer for long-range planning efforts, research projects, anything involving computers or systems design, as well as studying the field of apologetics.

INVESTIGATIVE LIFE GIFTS

Life Gifts	When have I used this? Or have I dreamed about using this?	How enjoyable were these experiences (1=terrible, 10=great)	How easy or difficult is it for me to use?	Could this be a life gift?
Inventing—to imagine or produce something useful, especially in technical, scientific, or theoretical realms				
Researching—investigating or experimenting to get information, examine theories, or find new applications of current knowledge				
Conceptualizing—originating and developing abstract ideas or theories				
Working independently—able to work well without guidance or input from others				
Solving complex problems—able to find solutions to difficult situations or unique issues, usually through logic or knowledge base				
Computer aptitude—adept at systems and software design and development				
Synthesizing information—organizing or combining information from different sources so that it is easily understood				
Theorizing—articulating explanations, finding connections, or projecting future trends				

The Artistic Type

General Description:

- **Original**—want to produce and be recognized for unique, distinctive works

- **Free-spirited**—are at their best in unstructured environments

- **Creative**—have imaginative personal perspectives and expressions

- **Artistic**—enjoy tasks that allow for use of aesthetic, musical, or verbal skills

Leisure pursuits for the Artistic mirror their life gifts. They especially enjoy listening to, seeing, or appreciating their own artistic gifts or those of others.

With these characteristics, Artistic types might volunteer for creative efforts or projects that involve music, drama, artwork, or decorating.

ARTISTIC LIFE GIFTS

Life Gifts	When have I used this? Or have I dreamed about using this?	How enjoyable were these experiences (1=terrible, 10=great)	How easy or difficult is it for me to use?	Could this be a life gift?
Acting—projecting emotions or character by performing roles, either formally in theater settings or informally				
Writing, reporting, technical writing—able to communicate clearly through written words, including reports, letters, and publications				
Verbal/linguistics skills—adept at studying or learning languages, using and comprehending spoken words				
Musical expression—able to compose music or perform musically, either with voice, body, or instruments				
Creative problem solving—able to find unusual solutions to issues, especially in artistic or interpersonal areas				
Sculpting/photography/graphic arts/painting—creative expression through artistic mediums				
Creative design through use of space—able to work with spatial concepts, as in interior design or architecture				
Creative expression through color—able to coordinate colors and patterns, as in clothing design, decorating, etc.				

The Social Type

General Description:

- **Helpful—offer assistance willingly for tasks and for aiding others in solving personal problems**
- **Cooperative—want to team with others rather than compete with them or do things alone**
- **Understanding—factor in their own and others' feelings, especially in decision making**
- **People-oriented—concerned for the ethical and responsible treatment of others**

In their spare time, many Socials choose to entertain friends or do volunteer work. Because Socials focus so heavily on the needs of people, which can be draining, they may choose Realistic or solitary activities for their leisure time to avoid burnout.

With these characteristics, Social types might volunteer for teaching, counseling, organizing social gatherings, small group leadership, or hospitality efforts.

SOCIAL LIFE GIFTS

Life Gifts	When have I used this? Or have I dreamed about using this?	How enjoyable were these experiences (1=terrible, 10=great)	How easy or difficult is it for me to use?	Could this be a life gift?
Teaching—instructing, demonstrating, training, or guiding the study of others so that they can learn facts or concepts				
Listening and facilitating—able to encourage others to volunteer information and discuss issues or topics, either one-on-one or in groups				
Understanding or counseling others—able to give appropriate advice and guidance tailored to the needs of others				
Conversing/informing—offering hospitality, talking and listening informally with one or a few others about daily events, issues, or personal concerns				
Being of service—considering and acting to aid the welfare of others				
Evaluating people's character—able to discern the motives and values of other people				
Being empathetic and tactful—aware of the feelings of others, able to adjust one's own behavior and respond accordingly				
Working with others—able to establish harmonious working relationships based on trust and synergy				

The Enterprising Type

General Description:

- **Persuasive—able to promote and sell ideas**
- **Self-confident—seek advancement and areas to be influential**
- **Outgoing—enjoy challenge, competition, and a fast-paced approach to life**
- **Risk-takers—prefer high visibility, ambitious goals, and ever-increasing responsibilities**

In their spare time, Enterprising types may pursue political activities or leadership in community organizations. They also enjoy social, sporting, and other events where they can see and be seen. The participative sports they choose—like tennis or golf—often reflect a desire to belong to prestigious clubs or social organizations.

With these characteristics, Enterprising types might volunteer for leadership, building campaigns, member involvement efforts, new ministry development, or evangelistic efforts.

ENTERPRISING LIFE GIFTS

Life Gifts	When have I used this? Or have I dreamed about using this?	How enjoyable were these experiences (1=terrible, 10=great)	How easy or difficult is it for me to use?	Could this be a life gift?
Public speaking—able to communicate clearly in front of a live audience				
Selling—able to convince others to purchase products or services				
Persuading—advocating the acceptance by others of ideas, values, or points of view				
Leadership—able to influence others to work together and direct people's efforts toward common missions or goals				
Management—planning, organizing and directing projects and resources to attain goals				
Negotiating—able to aid others in listening to diverse opinions or demands so as to reach agreement or compromise				
Taking action—responding decisively in emergency or stressful situations				
Adventurousness—able to take above-average financial and interpersonal risks				

The Conventional Type

General Description:

- **Practical**—apply tried and true methods to run things according to plan
- **Methodical**—establish and follow rules and procedures
- **Efficient**—use numerical skills, time management, and their eye for detail to provide stability
- **Orderly**—contribute consistency and accuracy to foster reliability

In their spare time, many Conventional types choose to vacation in familiar, restful places such as a family cabin or seaside resort where they can renew old acquaintances. They may enjoy hobbies such as china collecting, building detailed models such as railroads or doll houses, or home maintenance projects.

With these characteristics, Conventional types might volunteer for office tasks, financial management, standing committees, record-keeping, establishing procedures, or defined roles such as ushering or registration.

CONVENTIONAL LIFE GIFTS

Life Gifts	When have I used this? Or have I dreamed about using this?	How enjoyable were these experiences (1=terrible, 10=great)	How easy or difficult is it for me to use?	Could this be a life gift?
Organizing—able to arrange records, finances, offices, production lines, homes, etc., in a structured manner				
Appraising/evaluating—able to accurately estimate the value or significance of investments, antiques, real estate, business opportunities, etc.				
Attending to detail—aware of the small elements that make up the whole, as in printed words, administrative tasks, or the environment				
Managing time, setting priorities—arranging activities and schedules so that deadlines, appointments, and goals are consistently met				
Calculating and mathematical skills—adept at working with numbers and figures; adding, subtracting, multiplying, dividing				
Systematizing—classifying information or things for ease of use				
Persistence—exhibiting follow-through and patience when handling responsibilities				
Stewardship—conservative handling of money, data, things, and people				

Constructing a Life Gifts Sentence

Discovering your life gifts, a part of you since birth, is an exciting process for many people, but you may be asking, "Where do I go from here?" You can link your life gifts into a sentence or series of phrases that will not only help you remember what your life gifts are but see how they often work together.

List your life gifts below:

When you are at your best, which 2-3 of these life gifts are you using? In other words, which life gifts are central to who you are?

Which gifts are normally used first, defining your central life gifts?

Which gifts are typically used after the others are used?

Work with your list of life gifts to construct a statement that links them together into a coherent picture of what you do best. Write your sentence below.

Here's what we came up with as we did this exercise:

David's sentence:
I list, interview, investigate, and research in order to synthesize and organize information. I then take the information to teach, train, promote, persuade, speak, or act so that I might be of service to people, especially in terms of interpersonal risk.

Jane's sentence:
I am drawn to things that need to change and use my life gifts of researching, facilitating, synthesizing, writing, and teaching to creatively solve problems in service to others.

Sandra's sentence:
I am motivated by the desire that I and others have for personal and spiritual growth. I listen, facilitate, gather, and synthesize information to create a knowledge base from which I can empathize with people and their needs. I then teach, write, coach, and advocate in order to spark insights for myself and others that empower us to address those needs.

LifeKey 3

There are no second fiddles in God's orchestra.

While life gifts are given to all and cover most of the purposes of life—how we relate to other people, find our work, and fill our leisure hours—spiritual gifts allow us to be a part of purposes bigger than what we can do alone. They help us carry out work that God wants done.

LifeKeys contains full descriptions for each of the spiritual gifts as well as suggestions for developing the gifts you discover. As you work to identify your spiritual gifts, please keep the following principles in mind:

- *Your spiritual gifts were given to you for the benefit of other people, not solely for yourself.* These gifts are offered so that the body of Christ has what it needs to spread God's message of love. We are simply stewards of the gifts we are given. Whatever gifts we have are for the common good, not for our own glorification.

- *The spiritual gifts are given according to God's will, not because of some effort on our part.* Christian maturity is shown not by spiritual gifts, but by the fruit of the Spirit: love, joy, peace, patience, etc. Thus, incredibly gifted Christians can do amazingly irresponsible things. Instead of putting any gift or person who has a certain gift on a pedestal, look for people who use their gifts wisely and fruitfully, whatever they are.

- *Each of us has something to contribute to the purposes God wants accomplished.* If for some reason we choose not to use the gifts God gave us, the church will be less than it could have been. Therefore, every individual and their unique contributions count.

The inventories below are only a part of the process of discovering your gifts. In addition:

- Instead of completing the following inventory in order, start by reading and responding to the descriptions of spiritual gifts that seem most appealing, likely, or similar to your life gifts.

- Read the stories about each gift in *LifeKeys* or listen to how others have used these gifts. Do these examples sound like things you could do?

- Read the statements below for each of the gifts. Check ☑ the statements that apply to you.

- When you have read through the gift descriptions and checked those that describe you, then rate your endowment of each of these spiritual gifts as follows:

    5. This is definitely one of my spiritual gifts.
    4. This is probably one of my spiritual gifts.
    3. I am unsure—I need to learn more about this gift or experiment with ways to use this gift to find out if it is one of mine.
    2. This is probably not one of my gifts.
    1. This is definitely not one of my gifts.

____ Helps	____ Evangelism
____ Hospitality	____ Teaching
____ Mercy	____ Discernment
____ Faith	____ Knowledge
____ Giving	____ Prophecy
____ Leadership	____ Wisdom
____ Administration	____ Healing
____ Shepherding	____ Miracles
____ Encouragement/	____ Tongues
Counseling	____ Interpretation of
____ Apostleship	Tongues

Choose your top five spiritual gifts and record them on the "Putting It All Together" chart on pages 16-17.

HELPS: The ability to work alongside others, attaching spiritual value to practical, often behind-the-scenes tasks that sustain the body of Christ

☐ I tend to notice and assist with practical tasks that need to be done.

☐ As I do routine tasks, I feel a spiritual link to the ministries or people I serve.

☐ I would rather be responsible for set tasks than be involved in leadership.

☐ I prefer to work behind the scenes and often avoid public recognition for what I do.

☐ I receive satisfaction through quietly serving others.

☐ I enjoy working on odd jobs, often seeing a need and tending to it without being asked.

HOSPITALITY: The ability to provide a warm welcome for people that demonstrates God's love by providing food, shelter, or fellowship

☐ I am comfortable around strangers and care deeply about how my church welcomes them.

☐ I can make all kinds of people feel welcome.

☐ I enjoy providing a safe environment for those who are in need.

☐ I feel fulfilled when I can open my home to others for food and fellowship.

☐ I am more concerned with whether guests feel welcome than whether my house is in order.

☐ I love to create appealing, appropriate environments for people.

☐ I view relationships as opportunities to pass on God's love.

MERCY: The ability to perceive the suffering of others and comfort and minister effectively with empathy

☐ I get upset when people are hurt, displaced, or rejected and I want to reach out to them in their suffering.

☐ I enjoy finding ways to show others how much God loves them.

☐ I can frequently see how to help people and meet their needs.

☐ I can readily gain the confidence of those in need.

☐ I am able to empathize with hurting people and enter into their healing process.

☐ I tend to see each person as a life that matters to God and reach out to people who are avoided by others.

☐ I enjoy conveying the grace of God to those who feel guilt or shame.

FAITH: The ability to recognize what God wants accomplished as well as to sustain a stalwart belief that God will see it done despite what others perceive as barriers

☐ I firmly believe God is active in our lives.

☐ Sometimes I sense that God is orchestrating a project or idea. I find it easy to encourage and support it when others have doubts.

☐ I believe deeply in the power of prayer and am aware of God's presence in my life.

☐ I am able to believe that God is faithful, even in the face of seemingly insurmountable difficulties.

☐ People often tell me I am an "incurable optimist."

☐ My personal experiences help me believe in the power of faith.

GIVING: The ability to give of material wealth freely and with joy to further God's causes

☐ I often give generously and joyfully.

☐ I am resourceful in finding ways to free up my resources to benefit others.

☐ I feel a sense of ownership in the ministries and projects I support financially.

☐ I'd rather give anonymously, for the most part, unless my example might inspire others to be generous.

☐ I tend to manage my own money well, often basing financial decisions on what will be made available for giving.

☐ I feel comfortable and have success with approaching others to give of their resources.

LEADERSHIP: The ability to motivate, coordinate, and direct the efforts of others in doing God's work

☐ I can motivate others and get people to work together toward a common goal.

☐ I have enough confidence in my vision of what should be done to give direction to others.

☐ I frequently accept responsibility in group settings where leadership is required.

☐ People under my leadership sense that they are headed in a good direction.

☐ When necessary, I can make unpopular decisions and work through the disagreements that follow.

☐ I can see in advance what people can achieve.

ADMINISTRATION: The ability to organize information, events, or material to work efficiently for the body of Christ

☐ I like to organize facts, people, or events.

☐ When I am working on a project or event, it is easy for me to see the necessary steps in the process to solve potential problems.

☐ I tend to be frustrated when I see disorganization.

☐ I enjoy learning about management issues and how organizations function effectively.

☐ I enjoy using my life gifts of managing time and priorities *and/or* organization *and/or* financial management.

☐ I am generally careful and thorough in handling details.

SHEPHERDING: The ability to guide and care for other Christians as they experience spiritual growth

☐ I enjoy encouraging others to develop in their faith.

☐ I tend to think in terms of groups, teams, and task forces rather than individual personalities as I think about how I might help others.

☐ I have compassion for those who seem to be getting off track. I long to see them come back to the fold.

☐ I would enjoy nurturing and caring for a group of people over a period of time.

☐ I like to see people form long-term, in-depth spiritual relationships.

☐ I can often assess where a person is spiritually; I try to create or look for places where they can connect to enable them to take the next step.

ENCOURAGEMENT/COUNSELING : The ability to effectively listen to people, comforting and assisting them in moving toward psychological and relational wholeness

☐ People tell me that I am a good listener.

☐ Others seem to be comfortable approaching me with their problems.

☐ I often see attributes or gifts in others that they are slow to recognize for themselves.

☐ I am usually aware of the emotional state of people around me, whether they are content or whether something is bothering them.

☐ In stressful situations, I often find myself able to give perspective on what is positive in a way that others find helpful.

☐ I tend to have more faith in people than they have in themselves.

☐ I sympathize easily with others and am tolerant of their shortcomings, yet I enjoy helping people mature in their faith.

APOSTLESHIP: The ability to minister transculturally, starting new churches or ministries that impact multiple churches

☐ I am excited about working in multiple church settings and diverse religious communities.

☐ I am interested in how the Gospel can be brought to those who have never heard it.

☐ I am attracted to new ministries, churches, or settings (perhaps such as the inner city) where a whole new approach to evangelism or service is needed.

☐ Presenting the Gospel to a different culture or in a different language sounds enjoyable.

☐ The idea of living or visiting different places excites me.

☐ I have often envisioned myself as a missionary.

EVANGELISM: The ability to spread the Good News of Jesus Christ to those who don't know Him in a way that makes them respond in faith and discipleship

☐ I enjoy studying the questions that challenge Christianity.

☐ I frequently think about people who do not have a

faith commitment, wishing they could understand how my faith helps me.

☐ I look for ways that might help others understand the difference Christianity can make in their lives.

☐ I can see how people's needs can be met through the Christian faith.

☐ I can comfortably talk about my Christian faith with others in a way that makes them comfortable as well.

☐ I enjoy many friendships outside the faith community.

☐ I get excited about sharing God's Good News with others and am thrilled when they receive the forgiveness of God.

TEACHING: The ability to understand and communicate God's truths to others effectively—in ways that lead to applications in their lives

☐ I like gathering information and then effectively communicating it to others.

☐ I love to study the Bible. I receive new insights and understanding fairly easily and love to share them with people.

☐ When I listen to other teachers, I often think of alternative ways to present the materials.

☐ When I communicate what I have learned, others are motivated to learn more about the Bible and their faith in God.

☐ I want to relate God's truth to life in a way that helps people grow and develop.

☐ When I'm learning a spiritual truth, I automatically envision how to present the concept in a useful way to others.

DISCERNMENT: The ability to recognize what is of God and what is not of God

☐ I can generally rely on my first impressions of people and whether their motives or character are authentic. I tend to "know" where a person is coming from.

☐ I sometimes sense when something like a book or presentation will bring people closer to God—or cause them to be pushed away.

☐ In many situations, I find my gut reacting to the circumstance or atmosphere I am experiencing, whether good or bad.

☐ My mind tends to pick up on whether books or speakers are in line with truths as revealed in the Bible. Contradictions stand out to me.

☐ I can distinguish different, nongodly sources of spiritual energy.

KNOWLEDGE: The ability to understand, organize, and effectively use information, from either natural sources or the Holy Spirit directly, for the advancement of God's purposes

☐ It is easy for me to gather and analyze information for projects, ministries, or other causes within the body of Christ.

☐ I enjoy studying the Bible and other books to gain insights and background for God's Word.

☐ I can organize information well to pass on to others.

☐ I seem to understand how God acts in our lives.

☐ At times I find myself knowing information about a situation that has not been told to me by anyone else.

PROPHECY: The ability to proclaim God's truths in a way relevant to current situations and to envision how God would will things to change

☐ I often spot the differences between cultural trends and biblical truths.

☐ I tend to see or think of images that convey God's truth.

☐ To me, repentance, change, and challenge are a healthy part of our spiritual life. I am very aware of the future consequences of choosing one path or another.

☐ I listen carefully for what God wants me to say to others.

☐ When necessary, I am able to confront people with the truth of a situation.

☐ It saddens me when others ignore or take lightly life's problems.

☐ Often I can verbalize God's truths in situations where that truth is encouraging—or even where that truth is unpopular or difficult for listeners to accept.

WISDOM: The ability to understand and apply biblical and spiritual knowledge to complex, paradoxical, or other difficult situations

☐ It is easy for me to make practical applications of the truths found in the Bible, thinking through different courses of action and determining the best one.

(Continued on page 18)

Life Gifts

Workbook pages 4-10, *LifeKeys* pages 28-59

1.

2.

3.

4.

5.

My Passions

Workbook pages 27-30, *LifeKeys* pages 182-203

My Life Gift Sentence

Workbook page 11, *LifeKeys* pages 50-51

As I ref

LifeKeys pages 241-2

My Personality Type

Workbook pages 19-22, *LifeKeys* pages 125-163

____ ____ ____ ____

This means the atmospheres I prefer include:

All Together

on these pages I see my mission as...

Spiritual Gifts

A list of my gifts and how I can use them

Workbook pages 12-18, *LifeKeys* pages 60-123

1.

2.

3.

4.

5.

Date:

My Values

Workbook pages 23-26, *LifeKeys* pages 164-181 and appendix

1.

2.

3.

4.

5.

6.

7.

8.

- [ ] People often come to me for advice about personal and religious matters.
- [ ] I am known for my depth of understanding and insights into complex matters.
- [ ] I am often able to find a profoundly simple solution in the midst of a difficult situation.
- [ ] I have resolved paradoxes by cutting through to the essence of an issue, helping those involved see God's way in the midst of conflicting viewpoints.

HEALING: The ability to call on God for the curing of illness and the restoration of health in a supernatural way

- [ ] I am naturally drawn to those who are sick either in spirit or in body.
- [ ] Sometimes God seems to work through my prayers to bring physical, spiritual, relational, or emotional healing to others.
- [ ] I am aware of God's presence and try to follow God's guidance for how to pray in each situation where healing is desired.
- [ ] Often I can sense whether a person's problems are physical or emotional in origin.
- [ ] When petitions for healing are spoken, I find myself wanting to pray.

MIRACLES: The ability to call on God to do supernatural acts that glorify Him

- [ ] I find myself praying for things that are obviously beyond the natural capacity of people.
- [ ] I seek for God to be glorified however my prayers are answered.

- [ ] I have seen God perform supernatural acts when I have prayed for intervention.
- [ ] I have seen others accept the Christian faith through these displays of the impossible being accomplished.
- [ ] I have faith that miracles happen even today.

TONGUES: The ability to speak in a language, known or unknown to others, supernaturally

- [ ] Occasionally I have prayed in language(s) I have never before heard.
- [ ] Sometimes in prayer, my love for God or my burden for others is so strong that I have difficulty expressing myself in words.
- [ ] I have been inspired or have inspired others to step out in faith through the use of personal prayer languages.
- [ ] I find during worship that my tongue wants to express itself in syllables I do not understand.

INTERPRETATION OF TONGUES: The ability to interpret spiritual languages

- [ ] I can interpret the words of others who have spoken in languages ("tongues"), even though I have never before heard the languages.
- [ ] I understand how messages given through the use of tongues serve to glorify God or the church.
- [ ] When somebody speaks in tongues, I feel the Holy Spirit giving me the ability to interpret or speak.

LifeKey 4

If you know yourself, you can find your God-given place.

Each of us has natural preferences for how we approach life—how we are energized, how we take in information, how we make decisions, and how we orient our lives. Taken together, these preferences add up to your personality type—your essential nature.

To clarify this concept of preferences, try signing your name below with your *non-preferred* hand:

For most people, this feels unnatural, awkward, difficult, or time-consuming. Now write your name with your *preferred* hand.

Most people say that this feels natural, easy, and comfortable. These concepts apply to our psychological preferences as well—while we can learn to use any of the eight preferences, we *prefer* using the ones that are most natural to us. Our preferences are keys to places or atmospheres that appeal to us the most.

To help you understand your unique and inate per-

sonality, we use a theoretical construct based on Jungian psychology and popularized through the Myers-Briggs Type Indicator® (MBTI). Jung saw psychological type as a tool through which we can better understand ourselves and therefore deepen our spiritual side.

While the following exercise can help you identify your personality type, you may wish to use the MBTI, which is a thorough questionnaire designed to help you sort your preferences. For referral to a qualified MBTI practitioner, ask your seminar leader, pastor, local community education program, or call the publisher of the MBTI, Consulting Psychologists Press (800-624-1765).

EXTRAVERSION OR INTROVERSION

This preference pairing deals with how you are energized—either from the external world [E] or from the internal world [I]. This preference is not about how outgoing or shy you are. Check ✔ which statement from each pair describes you best:

Extraversion	Introversion
☐ Doing, lots going on	☐ Reflecting, one thing going on
☐ Find interruptions stimulating	☐ Find interruptions distracting
☐ Outgoing	☐ Protective
☐ Invite others in	☐ Wait to be invited
☐ Say what they're thinking	☐ Keep thoughts to themselves
☐ Outer energy	☐ Inner energy
☐ Act	☐ Reflect
☐ Live it first	☐ Understand it first
☐ Focus outside	☐ Focus inside
☐ Take over	☐ Take cover

Overall, the preference that describes me best is Extraversion (E) ____ or Introversion (I) ____

THINKING OR FEELING

This preference pairing deals with how you make decisions—by using objective, logical principles [T], or by considering the impact of each alternative on the people involved [F]. Check ✔ which statement from each pair describes you best:

Thinking	Feeling
☐ Logical, analytical	☐ Harmonious, personal
☐ Ideas for data and things	☐ Ideas for people
☐ Fair but firm— few exceptions	☐ Empathetic, making exceptions
☐ Business first	☐ Camaraderie first
☐ Recognition for exceeding requirements	☐ Praise for personal effort
☐ Analyze	☐ Sympathize
☐ Impartial	☐ Subjective
☐ Decide with head	☐ Decide with heart
☐ Find the flaw	☐ Find the positive
☐ Reasons	☐ Values

Overall, the preference that describes me best is Thinking (T) ____ or Feeling (F) ____

SENSING OR INTUITION

This preference pairing deals with how you gather information—through your five senses [S] or through hunches, analogies, and connections [N].[1] Check ✔ which statement from each pair describes you best:

Sensing	Intuition
☐ Practical, common sense	☐ Innovative, insightful
☐ Accuracy	☐ Creativity
☐ Use past experience for current work	☐ Use inspiration for current work
☐ Methodical approach	☐ Novel approach
☐ By (or buy!) the book	☐ Create the book
☐ Current reality	☐ Future possibilities
☐ Stick with it until you're done	☐ Stick with it until you find a better way
☐ Real world	☐ Ideal world
☐ Applied	☐ Theoretical
☐ Identify pieces	☐ Identify connections
☐ Seen	☐ Unseen

Overall, the preference that describes me best is Sensing (S) ____ or Intuition (N) ____

JUDGING OR PERCEIVING

This preference pairing deals with how you choose to approach your life—whether you plan your moves [J] or go with the flow [P]. Check ✔ which statement from each pair describes you best:

Judging	Perceiving
☐ Organized, efficient	☐ Flexible, multitask
☐ Planned events	☐ Serendipitous events
☐ Stress reduced by planning ahead	☐ Stress reduced by contingencies
☐ Settled and decided	☐ Open to late-breaking information
☐ Work before play	☐ Work and play coexist
☐ Regular, steady effort leads to accomplishment	☐ Much is accomplished through last-minute effort
☐ Systematic	☐ Spontaneous
☐ Scheduled	☐ Spur of the moment
☐ Definite selection	☐ Possible choices
☐ Enjoy finishing	☐ Enjoy starting

Overall, the preferences that describe me best are Judging (J) ____ or Perceiving (P) ____[2]

---

[1] Since the letter "I" is used for Introversion, "N" is used for INtuition

[2] Some of the descriptors in these lists reflect the contributions of Ken Green of Green Light Consulting, St. Paul, MN, and are used with his permission.

Record below the preferences that describe you best:

          ____   ____   ____   ____

          E or I   S or N   T or F   J or P

Through class discussion or as you read your type description (*LifeKeys* pp. 138-153), record your observations below.

What factors are important to you as you choose places or settings to work or serve?

In what ways, if any, does your current setting conflict with your type preferences? What actions can you take to change your current settings or your outlook toward them to be more aligned with your psychological type?

How can you honor your type and the person you are? How can you select future settings that work best for you?

The Sixteen Types at a Glance

ISTJ	ISFJ	INFJ	INTJ
• Contribute by being dutiful, hardworking, and conserving of tradition • Lead by focusing on what needs to be done to keep things "shipshape" • Serve in administrative areas, especially organizational, financial, record keeping [3]	• Contribute by offering sensible, matter-of-fact attention to people's daily needs • Lead by conscientiously organizing behind the scenes, enrolling others to accomplish tasks • Serve in office administration, data management, to provide practical help	• Contribute by lending future-oriented ideas, insights for people • Lead by inspiring with their goals, working for cooperation and mutual trust • Serve by small group leadership, using words, oral or written, to influence people's growth and development	• Contribute by breaking new ground, shifting paradigms, changing current perceptions • Lead by challenging and organizing to work toward a compelling future • Serve through finding and teaching about new approaches with wide ramifications
ISTP	**ISFP**	**INFP**	**INTP**
• Contribute by finding the best way to handle projects, using their storehouse of facts • Lead in a crisp, practical, efficient, hands-off style, unless the situation or people call for more • Serve in pragmatic, straightforward, and necessary projects or crises	• Contribute by giving immediate, direct, one-on-one help to people in need • Lead when they have the knowledge required, when no one else will, in a tolerant, flexible way • Serve through practical support: nursery or elder care, prayer and healing	• Contribute by reminding others of their ideals, providing a positive vision for the future • Lead by persuading through their convictions, inspiring others to do what is right • Serve in creative, artistic endeavors, providing one-to-one help	• Contribute by searching for truth, pointing out errors, providing clear, analytical frameworks • Lead by intellectual influence, winning respect through depth of knowledge • Serve through scholarly efforts: conceptualizing, reviewing, and developing programs
ESTP	**ESFP**	**ENFP**	**ENTP**
• Contribute by meeting practical needs efficiently, adding a "spark of life" to things they touch • Lead by bringing order out of chaos in the fastest, most direct way • Serve through activity-oriented, hands-on projects, often for crisis situations	• Contribute by adding warmth, excitement and fun to endeavors • Lead by attracting others through enthusiasm, energizing people to start a task • Serve through tangible acts of service, action-oriented projects and celebrations	• Contribute by adding vision and zest, especially in new undertakings • Lead by motivating and encouraging people through charisma and ingenious ideas • Serve by being liaisons to other organizations: evangelism, public speaking, promoting	• Contribute by enthusiastically initiating new programs, meeting challenges proactively • Lead by advocating change, organizing, assuming risks for new ideas • Serve through strategy development, marketing, and promoting to meet spiritual needs
ESTJ	**ESFJ**	**ENFJ**	**ENTJ**
• Contribute by using direct experience to organize for meeting current needs • Lead by marshaling people and tasks, focusing efforts to meet goals • Serve through direct, tangible management or administrative projects	• Contribute by knowing what matters for people and organizations • Lead in a take-charge yet caring style, building relationships while accomplishing tasks • Serve people directly through hospitality, visitation, organization, and administration	• Contribute by believing in people's positive nature, offering warmth and encouragement • Lead by planning for future needs of people, and large-scale endeavors • Serve through teaching, greeting, structuring, organizing activities and organizations for people	• Contribute by understanding how parts interrelate, then developing long-range plans • Lead by taking charge when a strong leader is needed, standing firm on principles • Serve in leadership, long-range planning, strategic alignment, and fund-raising

[3] The service areas listed for each type are examples of work that type might choose, not exhaustive lists

LifeKey 5

Seek the values that strike the right chord with God.

What do you value? Think of the things that...

...are important to you

...define your fundamental character

...supply meaning to your work and life

...influence the decisions you make

...compel you to take a stand

...provide an atmosphere in which you are most productive.

You may not know what you value until an event, circumstance, or person comes into direct conflict with that value—or until you purposefully try to identify what is important to you.

There are three ways to complete this values clarification exercise: The book *LifeKeys* includes a set of fifty-one values cards that you can sort and prioritize. You can make your own set using 3 x 5 cards or you can number the values listed on this page.

VALUES CLARIFICATION EXERCISE

Rate each of the values listed below as:

1. **This is very important to me**
   Limit yourself to eight values rated very important to you!

2. **This is important to me**

3. **This is not very important to me**

____ Accuracy	____ Learning
____ Achievement	____ Leisure
____ Advancement	____ Location
____ Adventure	____ Love
____ Aesthetics	____ Loyalty
____ Artistic Expression	____ Nature
____ Authenticity	____ Organization
____ Balance	____ Peace
____ Challenge	____ Perseverance
____ Competency	____ Personal Development
____ Competition	
____ Conformity	____ Physical Fitness & Health
____ Contribution	
____ Control	____ Power
____ Cooperation	____ Prestige
____ Creativity	____ Recognition
____ Efficiency	____ Religious Beliefs
____ Fairness	____ Responsibility
____ Family	____ Security
____ Financial Security	____ Self-Respect
____ Flexibility	____ Service
____ Friendship	____ Stability
____ Generosity	____ Tolerance
____ Happiness	____ Tradition
____ Humor	____ Variety
____ Independence	—— ————————
____ Influence	—— ————————
____ Integrity	—— ————————

Record your eight most important values:

Value	My definition
1.	
2.	
3.	
4.	
5.	
6.	
7.	
8.	

What are your thoughts about the values you selected? Are there any surprises?

VALUES APPLICATIONS
Listed below are several different questions to help you work with your values. Read through all of the questions. You need not do all of them, but choose those that are most appropriate for your current situation.

1. **To evaluate your current work/service environment:** List again your eight top values. Then review the list one more time to choose the eight values you believe are most important in your workplace. Are there any conflicts between the two lists? (Comparing lists of values can also be useful for husband/wife discussions or team building.)

2. **Does this exercise explain any of the conflict or tension you feel?** How might this be resolved? When conflict or tension exists, you may wish to talk through alternatives with a trusted person.

3. **To consider whether a job or service opportunity fits your values or what atmosphere is needed to harmonize with your values:** Assume that you have found a job or service opportunity that fits with your life gifts, spiritual gifts, personality type, and passions. What is the atmosphere needed for it to mesh with your top eight values?

MY NEXT SEASON OF LIFE

As you think about the next season of your life and how your values might change, define the next season of your life—new job, empty nest, end of school, retirement—whatever you believe your next stage will be. How do you think your values might change? Resort the values to find the top eight values for the next season of your life.

My next season of life will be _____.		
My current top values	My next season top values	My definition of this value
1.		
2.		
3.		
4.		
5.		
6.		
7.		
8.		

1. **What in your life will be difficult to control as your values change?**

2. **What areas of change will be stressful for you?** Are there any potential conflicts? What are two or three concrete steps you can take to move toward your next season values?

3. **How does this values clarification change your priorities regarding God, family, work, friends?** How can you maintain balance?

MORE VALUES EXERCISES

Use these questions to further clarify your values.

1. **From your outward actions, what might other people discern as your top values?** (A friend, co-worker, family member) Are there conflicts?

2. **Consider whether any of your top eight values are in conflict with one another.** For example, valuing financial independence and generosity at the same time can be problematic, as can valuing both adventure and stability!

3. **Pull out your calendar and think about the past week.** Write out your activities to see how they correspond to your top eight values. Consider any goals you would like to set to bring your lifestyle more in line with your values.

LifeKey 6

You are called to serve where you can harmonize with God's song in your heart.

Passions are desires or purposes that bring us joy. Webster's defines passion as a powerful emotion: "fervor, ardor, enthusiasm, zeal." The word "enthusiasm" comes from the Greek phrase *en theos,* "with God." Thus, if you are *enthusiastically* pursuing a passion that God has put in your heart, you are doing it *with God!*

People often begin to discern their passions through one of four approaches. Which approach sounds most like you?

- **The "One Talent" Approach**—do you look for chances to use a *specific* life gift or spiritual gift in a variety of arenas?

- **The "Make Me an Offer" Approach**—are there certain leaders or ministries with visions or missions that appeal to you? Are there roles to fill within those efforts that fit with your gifts?

- **The "Right Under Your Nose" Approach**—if you broaden your definition of passions, might yours appear right where you are, in the settings you enter regularly?

- **The "Dreamer" Approach**—do you find it easy and exciting to simply dream about what you might do for God in order to discover where to focus your efforts?

Below are questions for each approach. Start with the approach that is most like you.

FOR THE "ONE-TALENT" PEOPLE

The following list is meant to trigger your own thoughts. It is by no means exhaustive or all-inclusive—seriously try to think of *other* areas! Which skills might you enjoy using?

- ☐ Artistic expression
- ☐ Car repairs
- ☐ Carpentry
- ☐ Coaching athletics
- ☐ Computers
- ☐ Cooking
- ☐ Crafts
- ☐ Driving
- ☐ Financial planning/budgets
- ☐ Foreign languages
- ☐ Gardening
- ☐ General management
- ☐ Graphic arts
- ☐ Home repairs
- ☐ Interior design
- ☐ Investigating
- ☐ Mathematics
- ☐ Office administration
- ☐ Organizing events/ parties
- ☐ Photography
- ☐ Political pursuits
- ☐ Reading
- ☐ Research
- ☐ Sewing
- ☐ Speaking
- ☐ Storytelling
- ☐ Teaching
- ☐ Time management
- ☐ Word processing

Others:
- ☐ _____
- ☐ _____
- ☐ _____

Look back through prior experiences, your life gifts, and your spiritual gifts. Which are the most enjoyable for you to use? How could you put those gifts to use more regularly?

FOR THE "MAKE ME AN OFFER" PEOPLE

1. **Write down the passions or interests of people who are already *en theos* in the space below.** How could you help these people accomplish their dreams? (Keep in mind, however, that for some of you, the character of the person in charge of a project may be more important than the project itself.)

2. **Find out what ministries and missions your church or organization actively supports.** Which of these are of interest to you?

3. **Get a list of the most recent volunteer opportunities available at your church, organization, or at another ministry that seems appealing to you.** Review these and write down those that are of interest to you. If there is a volunteer notebook in existence (with descriptions of available opportunities), take time to review it for possibilities.

4. **Contact the formal or informal leadership of your spiritual community or organization in areas that seem attractive to you.** Examples: adult education, outreach, member involvement, music, etc. Ask them what needs they have for volunteers.

FOR THE "RIGHT UNDER YOUR NOSE" PEOPLE

1. **Which of these groups do you most easily relate to?** Who do you wish you could help, or feel drawn to because of personal experience or frequent encounters?

Age group:

- ☐ Children
- ☐ Teens
- ☐ College/young adults
- ☐ Singles
- ☐ Young marrieds
- ☐ Parents of young children
- ☐ Parents of teens
- ☐ People approaching mid-life
- ☐ Empty nesters
- ☐ Seniors

People with practical needs:

- ☐ Education (or tutoring)
- ☐ Finance/budget issues
- ☐ Nursing/healthcare assistance
- ☐ Housing needs
- ☐ Legal advice/concerns
- ☐ Maintenance or repair needs
- ☐ Parenting concerns
- ☐ Workplace issues
- ☐ Prayer ministries

People with counseling needs:

- ☐ Substance abuse
- ☐ Marital counseling
- ☐ Grief support
- ☐ Spiritual direction/ discipleship
- ☐ Families experiencing relationship problems
- ☐ Support groups

Ministries to specific populations:

- ☐ Business and professional men/ women
- ☐ Community/neighbors
- ☐ People with disabilities or illnesses
- ☐ Ethnic groups/refugees
- ☐ International students
- ☐ Missionaries
- ☐ New church members
- ☐ Unemployed
- ☐ The disenfranchised

Others:

2. **List below the roles you play or have played during the past three years.** Examples: employer, employee, parent, child, teacher, neighbor, citizen, patient, counselor, customer, etc. What concerns arose for you in those roles? Which ones could you act upon?

FOR THE "DREAMERS"

1. **If you had no fear of failure and limitless time and resources at your disposal, what would you do (after your trip around the world!)?** What are some of the longings of your heart that you would finally be able to address? What "dreams" continually cross your mind?

2. **Name three people who have accomplished something that you would like to do or who have had a tremendous positive impact on your life.** Because of them, toward what causes or purposes might you like to turn your efforts?

Name of person	What they did	What I might do
1.		
2.		
3.		

LIFEKEY #7

Keep in step with God's syncopation for YOUR life.

What does each of the five biblical principles for making life choices mean to you? Take a moment to rank the five principles in your own life, giving a "1" to the area you feel you manage best and a "5" to the area where you believe you could most improve. Where are you in control? What are your strengths? What don't you have time for? Record any insights for making better life choices.

My
Ranking   Biblical Principle

_____   **Put first things first—seek the kingdom of God**
           Do you successfully find time to pursue your own spiritual practices? If this is a struggle for you, check your personality type description (page 138-153 of *LifeKeys*) for "Possible Spiritual Helps" that might be appealing to you.

_____   **Know your mission**
           If you do not yet have a mission statement, construct one using the information from "Putting It All Together (pages 16-17) and the process outlined on pages 241-243 of *LifeKeys*.

_____   **Know your limits**
           Are you often scattered or exhausted? Make a list of the activities that *re-create* you or bring you rest—hobbies, sports, relationships, solitude, time in nature, etc. Do you find time for these? Remember that you may need to purposefully schedule your time for re-creation to avoid being drained by the urgent needs of each day.

_____   **Simplify—aim for balance in your life**
           Are you in control of your possessions and commitments or do they control you? Are there any that keep you from things you consider truly important? Do any take too much of your time in view of other priorities?

_____   **Reflect on people who seem to "have enough time"**
           If finding time to act on your passions seems impossible, consider how others manage to have enough time to act with God. Identify one step that you could commit to now or two or three *months* from now that would give you a chance to begin to work toward fulfilling the passions you identified through *LifeKeys*.

JANE A. G. KISE is a freelance writer and management consultant in the fields of strategic planning and team building. She holds a B.A. from Hamline University and an M.B.A. in finance from the University of Minnesota. She is the coauthor of a book on personality types at work.

DAVID STARK is a pastor at Christ Presbyterian Church in Edina, Minnesota, and founder and director of training for Church Innovations. His small-group materials, *People Together*, are widely used in churches in a variety of denominations. He holds an M.Div. from Princeton Theological Seminary and has led dozens of workshops and seminars throughout the United States.

SANDRA KREBS HIRSH is a management consultant, providing career management and organizational development consultation. She holds graduate degrees in American Studies and Industrial Relations. One of her books on the Myers-Briggs Type Indicator® has sold over a million copies. She is much in demand worldwide for her expertise in Human Resources and Organizational Development.

––––––––

For more information on how you can teach *LifeKeys* in your church, business, or other organization, or for information on *LifeKeys* training seminars, please write:

LifeKeys
1319 Preston Lane
Hopkins, MN 55343

or call:

(612) 935–7591